Meeting friends

1 Talk about the picture.

2 Listen to your teacher.
Point to the numbers.
Say the colours.

3 Listen. Where do they live?

Note

Auf dem Bild siehst du eine Straße in England. Was fällt dir auf?

Number … is Harry's house.

Door number 3 is yellow.

1

1 Listen. Point to the numbers.

2 Say the numbers.

3 Play 'hopscotch'.

You start, Emily.

1

1, 2, …

Good, Emily.

10, 9, 8, …

2

Oops!

3

4 Read the dialogue. Talk to a partner.

What's your favourite colour?

My favourite colour is green.

Sunshine

Pupil's Book 3

Erarbeitet von
Stefanie Aschkar (Konstanz)
Tanja Beattie (Ebersberg)
Nadine Kerler (Ulm)
Caroline Schröder (München)

Auf der Grundlage der Ausgabe von
Birgit Hollbrügge
und Ulrike Kraaz

Cornelsen

Contents

Symbols

listen to your partner or teacher

read

draw or write

listen to the CD, track 2

talk

extra

play

Getting started

📖 **1** Read the words:
computer, cowboy, mountain bike, skateboard.
Find the pictures.

📖 **2** Find more English words.

👂⭐ Listen to your partner. What shop is it?

1 Listen to the rhyme. Point to the pictures.

⭐ Say the rhyme with a partner. Do the actions.

1, 2,
how are you?

3, 4,
touch the floor.

5, 6,
no more tricks.

7, 8,
don't be late.

9, 10,
start again.

11, 12,
say it yourself.

1 Talk about Harry's family. Say: *This is …*

 2 Listen. Point to the pictures.

Let's talk

3 Read the dialogue. Talk to a partner.
⭐ More: Make up your own dialogue.

Have you got a sister?

No, I haven't. I've got a brother.

1 Look at the map. Where do they speak English?

Talk about the colours and the flags.

⭐ Listen to your partner. Point to the country.

🔍 **Note**

Where is Germany on the map?

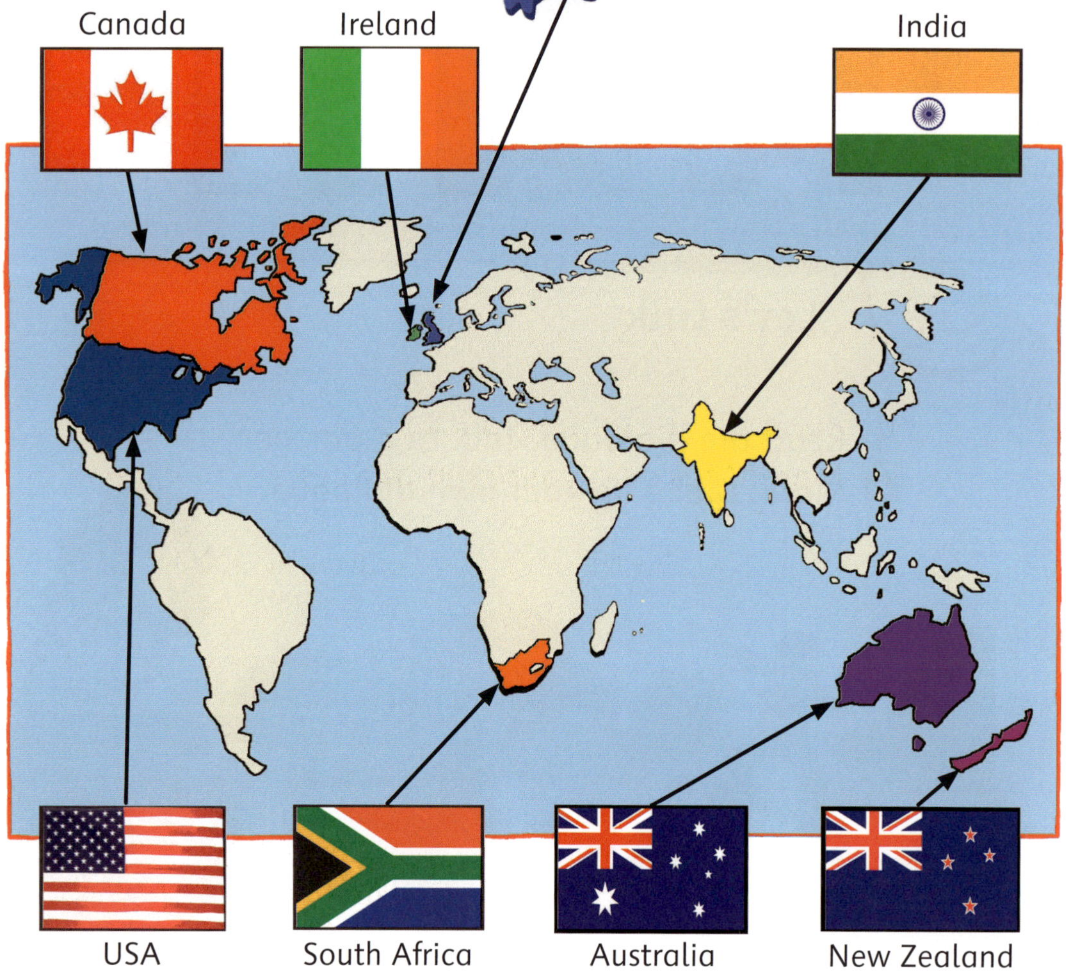

I'm from Great Britain. My flag is red, white and blue. What colour is your flag?

Canada

Ireland

India

USA

South Africa

Australia

New Zealand

1 Listen. Who is on the phone?

Hi, ...!

Let's talk

2 Read the dialogue. Talk to a partner.
⭐ More: Make up your own dialogue.

Hi Lisa.

Hi, Leon.

Can you come and play?

Yes, I can.

OK. See you. Bye.

See you. Bye-bye.

🗨 **1** Talk about the picture. What pets can you see?

📀 **2** Listen. What pets do the children have?

📖 ⭐ Read with a partner. What food do the pets like?

Story: **Rabbit's party**

1 Read the story.

2 Act out the story.

2

1 Read the words and sentences.

2 Talk about the rules.

3 Play the game.

Go to the matching picture.

Go to the matching word.

Take a card. Say a sentence.

Miss a turn.

START

dog

rabbit

apple

rat

cat

carrot

hamster

lettuce

guinea pig

peanuts

FINISH

 1 Listen. Point to the pictures.

sheep dog

rescue dog

police dog

guide dog

2 Read the speech bubbles with a partner.

3 Do the dog actions with your partner. Guess the actions. Take turns.

4 Play the game with your class.

1 Talk about the picture. Where's Mr Mole?

2 Listen to the song. Point to the school things in the picture.

⭐ Read the text with a partner.

> *Where's Mr Mole?*
> *Where can he be?*
> *Where's Mr Mole?*
> *Let me see.*
>
> *Is he in the school bag?*
> *Is he on the book?*
> *Or under the table?*
> *Let's have a look.*
>
> *No! Not there!*

1 Read the texts.

 2 Talk about the rules.

 3 Play the game in groups of 4.

① Take 5 cards from your word box.

② Put your cards on the table.

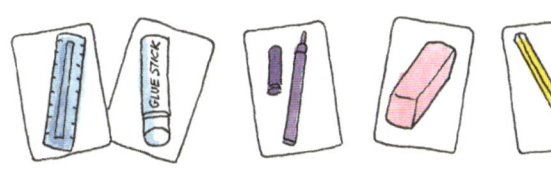

③ Shuffle all the cards.

④ Give 5 cards to each player.

⑤ Ask questions.

The player with the most cards wins.

Story: **Jack's bad day**

1 Listen to the story.

2 Read the story.

3 Act out the story.

Read the text.

That's my book. Give it back, Jack!

Draw an apple.

That's my pencil. Give it back, Jack!

Colour the apple red.

That's my felt tip. Give it back, Jack!

It's time for lunch.

Ouch!

That's my rat. Give it back, Jack!

 **Note**

In England schaust du zuerst nach rechts, wenn du eine Straße überquerst. Weißt du warum?

 1 Talk about the pictures.

 2 Listen. Point to the pictures.

 3 Read the texts.

A **lollipop man** helps children cross the road.

Some children walk to school with the **walking bus**.

This is a **school building**.

School starts with **assembly**.

 4 Make a school badge. You need:

cardboard	felt tips or coloured pencils	scissors	a safety pin	sticky tape

1. Draw a circle on the cardboard. Write your school's name. Colour the badge.

2. Cut out the badge.

3. Tape a safety pin to the back of your badge.

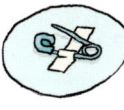

Watch the film.

 4

4 The second-hand shop

1 Talk about the picture. Say: *I can see …*

⭐ Listen to your partner.
Find the clothes in the picture.

I can see …

pullover   trousers   dress   skirt   shoes

❗ Note

🇬🇧   🇩🇪

jeans – Jeans

Can you find more words that are the same in German and English?

1 Listen to your teacher. Who is it?

2 Play 'I spy'.

She is wearing a red dress. Who is it?

It's …

Note

she = girl

he = boy

1 Sarah

2 Harry

3 Kate

4 Samir

5 Emily

6 John

Let's talk

1 Read the dialogue. Talk to a partner.
⭐ More: Make up your own dialogue.

2 Talk to your partner. Ask: *Do you like ...?*

Story: **A funny boy**

1 Read the story.

2 Act out the story.

Can I have the shirt, please?

The pink shirt?

Yes, I like pink.

The shirt is too big.

That's OK. I like the shirt.

Can I have the shoes, please?

The green shoes?

Yes, I like green.

Your feet are too small!

No, the shoes are too big. But that's OK.

He's so funny.

You're funny.

That's good. I'm the clown in our school play.

Story: **The smartest giant in town**

 1 Listen to the story. Point to the pictures.

 2 Talk about the pictures. How does the story end?

① ② ③

④ ⑤ ⑥

 ⭐ Read the rhyme with a partner.

Find the matching pictures.

What about picture 6?

> My tie is a scarf for a cold giraffe.
>
> My shirt's on a boat as a sail for a goat.
>
> My shoe is a house for a little white mouse.
>
> One of my socks is a bed for a fox.
>
> My belt helped a dog who was crossing a bog.

> **! Note**
>
> Find the rhyming words.
> boat – goat
> ...
> Make a list.

More to explore: **School uniforms**

1 Talk about school uniforms. What is the boy wearing?
What is the girl wearing? Say: *The girl is wearing …*

> a cardigan · a pullover ·
> a shirt · shoes · a skirt ·
> socks · a tie · trousers

Note

In Großbritannien tragen
die Kinder Uniformen in
der Schule.
Wie findest du das?
Begründe!

2 Listen. Point to the pictures.

★ Listen to your partner. What school is it?

①

②

③

Watch
the film.

| Queen's School | Swanage School | Blake School |

5 Free-time activities

1 Listen to the song. Point to the pictures.

2 Sing the song.

⭐ Talk to a partner. Make up your own song.

Football, music, books, TV
Bikes and comics, friends, PC
Tell me, tell me,
What about you?
Do you like the things I do?

Playing football
Is what I like
Watching TV
Riding my bike.

Listening to music
Tapping my feet
Meeting friends
In the street.

Reading books
And comics, too
Playing computer games.
What about you?

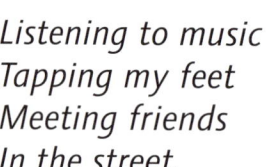

I like meeting friends. What do you like?

Let's talk

1 Read the dialogue. Talk to a partner.
⭐ More: Make up your own dialogue.

What about listening to music?

Great idea!

That's boring.

2 Listen to the rhyme. Point to the pictures.

3 Read the rhyme.

⭐ Make up your own rhyme. *Is it in …?*

Words for your rhyme:

ball · garden shed · painting · playing · toilet · wall

Where's the cat? Where's the cat?
Is it in the living room – watching TV?
Is it in the kitchen – drinking my tea?

Where's the cat? Where's the cat?
Is it in the bedroom – eating my shoe?
Is it in the bathroom – playing with shampoo?

Where's the cat? Where's the cat?
There it is – sleeping in Mum's favourite hat.

1 Look at the pictures. Where's Harry?

⭐ Listen to your partner. Find the things in the pictures.

①

②

Story: **The babysitters**

1 Listen to the story.
Point to the pictures.

2 Read the story.

1 Oh, this is boring.

2 Here's a great CD.

I don't like listening to music.

3 What about playing football?

Great idea! Where's my football?

4 Is your football in your bedroom?

No, it isn't in my bedroom.

5 Not in the living room, Nick!

Oh dear. Sorry!

3 Listen to the story. What don't they say?

1 What about meeting friends?

2 What about playing computer games?

3 What about watching TV?

More to explore: **Rhymes and playground games**

  **1** Look at the pictures.
Read the names of the games.

2 Talk about the games.

3 Listen. Point to the pictures.

LISA

SALLY

PAUL

SAM

 **4** Read the rules. Talk about the rules.

 **5** Play 'rock, paper, scissors'.

Note

Was spielst du gerne auf dem Schulhof? Vergleiche.

① Say and do.　② Who's the winner?　③ Two hands the same?

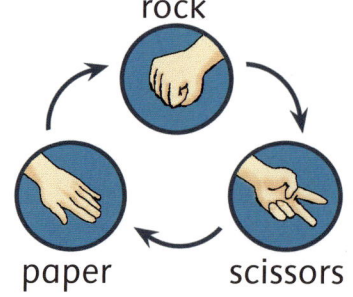

Rock, paper, scissors. Show!

rock

paper　　scissors

Play again!

1 Talk about the picture. Where is Mr Mole?

2 Listen to your teacher. Find the numbers.

⭐ Talk to a partner.
How many dogs / tables / scooters / … can you see?
Say: *I can see …*

6

1 Talk about the picture. Say: *How much is ...? – It's ...*

2 Listen. What does the boy say?

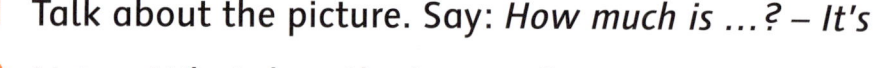

I'd like ...

Let's talk

3 Read the dialogue. Talk to a partner.

⭐ More: Make up your own dialogue.

Hi, can I help you?

I'd like a strawberry special. How much is it?

It's £1.50. Anything else?

No, thank you.

Story: **Where's my ice cream?**

1 Listen to the story.

2 Read the speech bubbles.
Say what's right and what's wrong.

More to explore: **Signs in the park**

 **1** Look at the signs. Read the sentences. Match.

2 Talk about the signs.

 Draw a new park sign.

Wheelchair access.	No ball games.
Please keep off the grass.	No bikes.

No horse riding.

No dogs.

Can you dig holes in the park?

Watch the film.

1 Talk about the picture.

2 Whose birthday is it today? Sing the song.

3 Listen to the song. Point to the pictures.

Someone's birthday is today, is today, is today.
Someone's birthday is today, and it's our …

Let's prepare a birthday cake,
birthday cake, birthday cake.
Let's prepare a birthday cake,
Just for our …

Add a candle for each year,
For each year, for each year.
Add a candle for each year,
Just for our …

Make a special birthday card,
Birthday card, birthday card.
Make a special birthday card,
Just for our …

 Note

Zum Geburtstag tragen englische Kinder gerne selbst gebastelte Hüte oder Kronen. Wie feierst du deinen Geburtstag?

Happy Birthday!

1 Look at the picture. Talk about the Christmas things.

2 Look at the pictures. Find the Christmas things in the house.

Special days: **Valentine's Day**

🔍 **Note**

When is
Valentine's Day?
Find out more.

1 Read the card.

Moles are cool

Moles are clever

I will love you

forever and ever

From **?**

2 Read the story with a partner.

⭐ **Present it in class.**

The world's smallest Valentine

It's Valentine's Day.
Olivia is visiting her granddad
and grandma.

Olivia: This is for you, Granddad.
Granddad: Oh, thank you. What is it?
Olivia: It's a Valentine card.
Granddad: What's inside the card?
Olivia: A tomato seed.
Granddad: A tomato seed?
Olivia: Yes. The old name for tomato is 'love apple'.
Granddad: Thank you, Olivia. A love apple seed.
What a lovely Valentine!

Special days: **Easter**

1 Listen to the rhyme.

2 Say the rhyme and do the actions.

Here is a bunny
with ears so funny,

And here is his hole in the ground.

When a noise he hears,
he pricks up his ears,

And hops in his hole in the ground.

I love
hot cross buns.

Word list

A

apple Apfel

B

banana Banane
bedroom Schlafzimmer
behind hinter
big groß
bike Fahrrad
birthday Geburtstag
birthday cake Geburtstagskuchen
birthday card Geburtstagskarte
birthday present Geburtstagsgeschenk
black schwarz
blackboard Tafel
blue blau
book Buch
boring langweilig
boy Junge
bread Brot
brother Bruder
brown braun
bye tschüss

C

can können
candle Kerze
carrot Möhre
cat Katze
chair Stuhl
cherry Kirsche
chocolate Schokolade
Christmas Weihnachten
Christmas Day Weihnachtstag (25.12.)
Christmas Eve Heiligabend (24.12.)
Christmas tree Weihnachtsbaum
class Klasse
classroom Klassenzimmer
cold kalt
colour Farbe, ausmalen
come kommen

D

dog Hund
draw zeichnen
dress Kleid, ankleiden
drink Getränk, trinken

E

Easter Ostern
Easter basket Osterkorb
Easter bunny Osterhase
Easter egg Osterei
eat essen
eight acht
eighty achtzig

F

family Familie
father Vater
Father Christmas Weihnachtsmann
favourite Lieblings-
felt tip Filzstift
fifty fünfzig
fish Fisch
five fünf
food Essen
football Fußball
forty vierzig
four vier
friend Freund
fruit Obst

G

garden shed Gartenhaus
girl Mädchen
gloves Handschuhe
glue stick Klebstift
good gut
great toll
green grün
grey grau
guinea pig Meerschweinchen

H

hamster Hamster
happy glücklich
hat Mütze
here hier
hobby Hobby
house Haus

I

ice cream Eiscreme
in in
in front of vor
in-line skates Inlineskates

J

jacket Jacke
jeans Jeans
juice Saft

L

lemon Zitrone
lettuce (Kopf-) Salat
like mögen
listening to music Musik hören
living room Wohnzimmer
lunch Mittagessen
lunch box Brotdose

M

meeting friends Freunde treffen
Merry Christmas!
  Frohe Weihnachten!
milk Milch
mother Mutter
mouse Maus

N

next to neben
nine neun
ninety neunzig
number Zahl

O

on auf
one eins
orange orange, Apfelsine

P

peach Pfirsich
peanuts Erdnüsse
pen Füller
pencil Bleistift
pencil case Federmappe
pencil sharpener Bleistiftspitzer
pet Haustier
pink rosa
play spielen
playing computer games
  Computerspiele spielen
playing football Fußball spielen
plum Pflaume
pound (£) Pfund (britisches Geld)
pullover Pullover

R

rabbit Kaninchen
rat Ratte
read lesen
red rot
reindeer Rentier

room Zimmer
rubber Radiergummi
ruler Lineal

S

scarf Schal
school Schule
school bag Schultasche
school bus Schulbus
scissors Schere
scooter Roller
seven sieben
seventy siebzig
shirt Hemd
shoes Schuhe
shop Laden
sister Schwester
six sechs
sixty sechzig
skateboard Skateboard
skirt Rock
small klein
snowboard Snowboard
socks Socken
stocking Strumpf
strawberry Erdbeere

T

T-shirt T-Shirt
teacher Lehrer, Lehrerin
ten zehn
thirty dreißig
three drei
tomato Tomate
trousers Hose
twenty zwanzig
two zwei

U

under unter

V

very sehr

W

watching TV fernsehen
white weiß

Y

yellow gelb

Word list

A

acht eight
achtzig eighty
ankleiden dress
Apfel apple
Apfelsine orange
auf on
ausmalen colour

B

Banane banana
blau blue
Bleistift pencil
Bleistiftspitzer pencil sharpener
braun brown
Brot bread
Brotdose lunch box
Bruder brother
Buch book

C

Computerspiele spielen
 playing computer games

D

drei three
dreißig thirty

E

eins one
Eiscreme ice cream
Erdbeere strawberry
Erdnüsse peanuts
essen eat
Essen food

F

Fahrrad bike
Familie family
Farbe colour
Federmappe pencil case
fernsehen watching TV
Filzstift felt tip
Fisch fish
Freund friend
Freunde treffen meeting friends
Frohe Weihnachten! Merry Christmas!
Füller pen
fünf five
fünfzig fifty
Fußball football
Fußball spielen playing football

G

Gartenhaus garden shed
Geburtstag birthday
Geburtstagsgeschenk birthday present
Geburtstagskarte birthday card
Geburtstagskuchen birthday cake
gelb yellow
Getränk drink
glücklich happy
grau grey
groß big
grün green
gut good

H

Hamster hamster
Handschuhe gloves
Haus house
Haustier pet
Heiligabend (24.12.) Christmas Eve
Hemd shirt
hier here
hinter behind
Hobby hobby
Hose trousers
Hund dog
hundert hundred

I

in in
Inlineskates in-line skates

J

Jacke jacket
Jeans jeans
Junge boy

K

kalt cold
Kaninchen rabbit
Katze cat
Kerze candle
Kirsche cherry
Klasse class
Klassenzimmer classroom
Klebestift glue stick
Kleid dress
klein small
kommen come
können can

Word list

L
Laden shop
langweilig boring
Lehrer, Lehrerin teacher
lesen read
Lieblings- favourite
Lineal ruler

M
Mädchen girl
Maus mouse
Meerschweinchen guinea pig
Milch milk
Mittagessen lunch
mögen like
Möhre carrot
Musik hören listening to music
Mutter mother
Mütze hat

N
neben next to
neun nine
neunzig ninety

O
Obst fruit
Orange, orange orange
Osterei Easter egg
Osterhase Easter bunny
Osterkorb Easter basket
Ostern Easter

P
Pfirsich peach
Pflaume plum
Pfund (£) pound
Pullover pullover

R
Radiergummi rubber
Ratte rat
Rentier reindeer
Rock skirt
Roller scooter
rosa pink
rot red

S
Saft juice
(Kopf-) Salat lettuce
Schal scarf
Schere scissors

Schlafzimmer bedroom
Schokolade chocolate
Schuhe shoes
Schulbus school bus
Schule school
Schultasche school bag
schwarz black
Schwester sister
sechs six
sechzig sixty
sehr very
sieben seven
siebzig seventy
Skateboard skateboard
Snowboard snowboard
Socken socks
spielen play
Strumpf stocking
Stuhl chair

T
T-Shirt T-shirt
Tafel blackboard
toll great
Tomate tomato
trinken drink
tschüss bye

U
unter under

V
Vater father
vier four
vierzig forty
vor in front of

W
Weihnachten Christmas
Weihnachtsbaum Christmas tree
Weihnachtsmann Father Christmas
Weihnachtstag (25.12.) Christmas Day
weiß white
Wohnzimmer living room

Z
Zahl number
zehn ten
zeichnen draw
Zimmer room
Zitrone lemon
zwanzig twenty
zwei two